TEXT: Henrique Urbano.
PHOTOGRAPHY: Neus Escandell-Tur and Alexandra Arellano.
COLLABORATION IN PHOTOGRAPHY: César Vivanco (p. 13; p. 20-f. 2; p. 22-f. 2; p. 35-f. 2).
Promperú (p. 17-f. 2; p. 22-f. 1; p. 35-f. 1; p. 39; p. 56-f. 2).
Oivind Tjelta (p. 4; p. 6; p. 9; p. 18-f. 2; p. 19-f. 1).
Documentary Compilation: Pilar Trujillo.
English translation: Lillian Valdés.

Photoset, photomechanism, printing and binding: Fisa Escudo de Oro, S. A.
Distribution: Tierra Firme Ediciones. Apartado 27-042, Lima 27. Tel. and Fax 440 24 79. E-mail: tfe@blockbuster.com.pe

ISBN 84-378-2141-X
Legal Dep.: B. 20650-2001

ALL MACHU PICCHU

Text:
Henrique Urbano

Photography:
Neus Escandell-Tur and Alexandra Arellano

TIERRA
FIRME
EDICIONES S.A.C.

Editorial Escudo de Oro, S.A.

The horizon visible in this scene might be considered as the symbol of Machu Picchu. In the 1920's, the eye of the great photographer from Cuzco, Martín Chambi, captured an initial glimpse of the spectacular unit formed by the settlements of the citadel and the hills which support this structure, surrounded and protected by the landscape which gives the area an unmistakable and majestic air. Here lie the peaks of the mountain range which the pre-Hispanic men adored and considered sacred beings and protectors.

«Then I have climbed up the steps of the land
through the dreadful thicket of the lost forests
to you, Machu Picchu.
High city of ascending stones,
final resting place from which the earthly
did not hide in their weary garments.
With you, as two parallel lines,
the cradle of lightning and of man
rocks to and fro in a wind of thorns».
(Pablo Neruda, p. 29).

1. Machu Picchu: an unexpected reencounter

Hiram Bingham visited Peru to find the «last refuge of the incas». When he arrived to Cuzco, he met Albert A. Giesecke, who introduced him into the social and intelectual circles of the City's society. Giesecke also introduced him to Melchor Arteaga, a peasant of the region who had offered to take him to Machu Picchu.

Together national and foreign professionals and institutions made the identification of the archaeological site of Machu Picchu possible on July 24, 1911, around 100 km northeast of Cuzco. People of the region already knew about it –Agustín Lizarraga had visited the ruins in 1902– but Bingham and Giesecke discovered it for the world.

This was the starting point of an undertaking which, up until today, continues to evoke admiration throughout the world. The impressive physical surroundings, with the silent presence of the snow-capped peaks and the lulling sound of the deep raging waters of the Aobamba and Urubamba rivers transformed the stones, the walls and what remains of the former Inca structures into a place which many associate with mysterious resonances and

Hiram Bingham: American explorer, professor of Southamerican History at Yale University. He raised the funds to work in the archaeological complex of Machu Picchu from Yale, from former students, as well as from his personal fortune. In the photograph, Bingham with his wife Susan dressed as a mestiza or «cholita».

Albert A. Giesecke: American professor graduated from Cornell, responsible of the educational reform in Peru conducted by President Leguia. At the time of Machu Picchu's descovery he was the Principal of the University of San Antonio Abad in Cuzco.
In the photograph, Giesecke riding a mule in a location on the mountain summit, probably linked to Machu Picchu. This was the way to reach the distant archaeological sites wich were covered by lush vegetation.

The sensation of peace and harmony among the inert rocky mass and the citadel which extends out from shape of the hill comes from the indelible line which marks the contours nature drew during the silence of the millenniums which preceded the arrival of man to these regions.

Through one's eyes enters the nearly obsessive presence of the peaks of Machu Picchu and the unmistakable beauty of Huayna Picchu, which looks over man and his works with a vigilant gaze, warm and compassionate:

«Mother of stone, froth of the condors.
high reef of the human dawn».
(Pablo Neruda, p. 29).

an aura of heavenly scenery. The force and power of attraction would have no explanation if it were a simple archaeological testimony. There is something more in the place and the scenery which makes Machu Picchu one of the most fascinating places on the American continent.

A silent story

Part of the fascination felt by visitors who discover the scenery of Machu Picchu is due to the lack of accurate information on the origin of the place and, therefore, on the reasons why the Inca decided to occupy and settle this area. One's imagination can wander freely among the walls and ancient structures and gaze at the hot, humid surroundings which extend towards a virgin wood. The testimonies are eloquent. Nobody can escape from the feeling of being in a marvelous world with an exceptionally rich and varied nature. Also, one can not help but suspect that, although there are no documents which verify such events, something important occurred in this place during the Inca period. The past is covered with a mantle of mystery.

A few years ago, some papers from the 16th century were revealed which refer to the existence of this region and the presence of pre-Hispanic ruins. Up until that time, there were testimonies by 19th century travelers, including the Frenchman Charles Wiener and the Italian Antonio Raimondi, who had pointed out the existence of important archaeological ruins in the area. But up until the time of the arrival of Bingham there were no reports from explorers who had bothered to recognize and study them.

Based on the general inventory of what is presently known about the place and the surrounding area, what is most important is the documentation of a hacienda which belonged to the Augustinian friars who received these lands as an inheritance in the 16th century. They had

Each morning the frequent and abundant clouds in the area seem to bathe the face of the rocks and peaks of the Ancient and Young Picchu –Machu and Huayna– leaving them with the humidity and heat of the water which returns to the forest:

«I gaze at the garments and the hands, the vestiges of water in the resounding cavity, the wall softened by the touch of a face which gazed with my eyes at the earthly lamps, which oiled with my hands the wood which has disappeared: because everything, clothing, skin, vessels, words, wine, bread, has been extinguished, has fallen to earth». (Pablo Neruda, pp. 29-30).

The terraces, the walls and footpaths are like tattoos on the body of the mountain. The geometry of the shapes dominates the hills as though those who inhabited the Andes had woven in the rock, with threads lengthened by the assembly of rocks and walls, their dreams and fantasies.

The design which the hills trace on the horizon blinds one's eyes and becomes an unforgettable image. As though it were prolonging the body of the bony mass of the rock, here lies the strange figure of Huayna-Picchu, millenary presence, imposing and hieratic. The Incas sought refuge here and they undoubtedly considered it a lord and protector.

been the witnesses of the life and death of the final Incas. They also lived with the Incas in this region and undoubtedly were familiar with these landscapes and structures, as well as those which the Inca chose further within the wood for their refuge and that of their loyal subjects, known with the name of Vilcabamba. The Augustinians attended the conversations held between the Spanish emissaries who attempted to demand the submission of the Incas and win them over to the Spanish crown and Roman Catholicism. The tension experienced by the Incas, who were under siege from the Spanish expeditions, affected the relationship between the friars and the native masters. In the midst of such conflicts, the lack of understanding between the two bands led some friars to pay with their lives. For all of these reasons, the presence of the Order of St Augustine in the region continued up until the 19th century, when the members of this religious order left Cuzco. Their goods and lands were sold or purchased by private parties or by the State.

Through the Augustinian friars and the documents which they left behind, we know that agricultural activities were conducted on vast expanses of land in the area during the colonial period. However, such records fail to mention the presence of significant pre-Hispanic structures in the Machu Picchu area. Of course the people in the settlements were not concerned with such matters. The friars were interested in the income from the lands and the native labor force. These were not times to think of increasing the archaeological heritage by a few more stones, much less based on lands which were considered isolated and far off from the point of view of the inhabitants of the city of Cuzco.

The Incas were finally subdued when Tupac Amaru was executed by order of the Viceroy Francisco Toledo in 1572. The references to Picchu which can be found in 16th century documents were erased from the memory of those who played a leading role in the colonial history of Cuzco. The tax records of the Augustinian friars are the only testimony of the existence of these stones which conserve the mystery and charm of pre-Hispanic life in the region. Bingham had not seen such records.

Reconstruction of the historic memory

Due to the circumstances in which the discovery by Bingham took place, the importance of Machu Picchu was only gradually recognized. In 1911 there was only one bridle path which led to the nearby outlying areas. The work performed in building a railway line from Cuzco began in 1913. This line finally reached the region of Machu Picchu, via Aguas Calientes, in 1928, and continued to the final destination on its route, Quillabamba. In the initial excavations Bingham reached the area by a road which was cleared in 1909. From this point he began to explore the region described in his work up until 1915. These were years of successive discoveries. But above all they were months and months of arduous physical work. The neglect and undergrowth which the structures had undergone damaged the area. Furthermore, the climate and the heavy rains erased important testimonies of their former inhabitants. Therefore, it is not surprising that little is known and much remains to be discovered and reconstructed.

The limited testimonies regarding Machu Picchu have led to an endless number of popular stories about the area. Explorers, travelers, historians and archaeologists have also attempted to determine the reasons for what has been discovered and to reconstruct a memory which is difficult to determine with certainty. Nevertheless, in recent years, more specifically in the 1970's, studies and documents, supported by well planned and demanding expeditions, have allowed the historian Edmundo Guillén to finally discard with certainty the statements made by Bingham which considered Machu Picchu as the «final refuge of the Inca rebels». During the years in which they sought refuge from the Spanish siege, the final Inca leaders lived in an area which was much further inland, known presently as Espíritu Pampa. Here the Incas, and with them the Augustinian friars, spent their final days.

What is not known with full accuracy is when the Incas settled in the region. There are indications that the Inca Pachacuti era could have been the period in which the Incas moved towards the Machu Picchu area. The name of Inca Pachacuti is always associated with the Inca presence throughout the Andes. This figure can be dated in the mid or latter part of the 15th century, perhaps approximately forty or fifty years before the Spaniards began to control the Andean region. Machu Picchu is considered to be one of these occupied lands. The valleys near the city of Cuzco, especially the Yucay valley, with the lands of Urubamba and Ollantaytambo, are regions which marked the point of entry for Inca colonization of the summit and the forest. Machu Picchu could have served as an excellent and quite suitable port of entry.

It is very difficult to speak with full historical accuracy about the settlements which existed before Pachacuti Inca. The mythical tales compiled by chroniclers of the sixteenth and seventeenth centuries mention Inca expansion towards the Cuzco valley before there was a clear desire to go beyond the nearby boundary of the natural city limits. In this sense, Viracocha Inca, who preceded Pachacuti Inca, seemed to have been interested in the occupation of the lands further north of the city, facing the Yucay and Urubamba valleys. With no further possibilities of verifying such information, what is true is that Machu Picchu as well as the structures found in Ollantaytambo were built on dates not far from the time when the Spaniards arrived in the city of Cuzco. Because of its size and the meticulous finishing of the

The cut of the walls on the hillside under the gaze of the peaks emphasizes the image of protection of the hills, where the ancient people sought refuge. They called them lords; in quechua, apu. The constructions are like rough masses in the womb of the mountain.

structures in Machu Picchu, it is believed that the Inca settlement formed as a result of this desire to occupy the area represented a major element in the political and economic structure which the Incas developed with evident intentions of exercising their power on the hottest lands of the summit as well as in the forest. Fruit and tubers, exotic animals and game came from this region. It is also quite likely that coca played an important role in the contacts established between Cuzco and the hotter, lower lands. There were also silver mines in the area, which were highly valued by the Incas. All of these facts justify the political project which led the Incas to expand their dominion over the Andes. There is no need to recur to reasons of an esoteric or religious nature to explain the Inca presence in the region.

A mystical and esoteric sacred place

Nevertheless, in recent years, the attraction which esoteric religions and practices have for an increasing group of supporters, have also reached Machu Picchu. International meetings held in the area have spread news of the strange sensations they felt while in this area next to the hundred-year-old stones. Participants recount that mystical and spiritual forces inhabit the area. Reviving such spirits is the dream of this growing number of followers of religious esotericism who seek to experience in their own flesh the mystical moments of the years when the Incas resided in Machu Picchu. This idea is compatible with the opinion expressed by some historians and archaeologists. All of them insist on the religious nature of Inca expansion, and that Machu Picchu was one of its manifestations.

The wonderful scenery and the beauty of the physical surroundings in the area do not contradict such ideas. The renowned Chilean poet Pablo Neruda dedicated a long poem to this area. The force of his poetry undoubtedly contributed to spreading the mystical dimension associated with Machu Picchu. His verses also express a vast political project in favor of Latin American unity. In this project, Machu Picchu is the beacon of continental fraternity, the region where the American lands collect light and energy to demonstrate to the world their cultural wealth and the spirit which animates them. The poetry of Neruda has religious resonances. It is not rare to find visitors meditating on these lines as they gaze at the hills, their eyes set on the dense green of the wood, imagining what the silent stones of the place conceal.

To state that Machu Picchu was a sacred place for the Incas is not completely unbelievable. Nevertheless, it would seem more accurate to state that such a large settlement, inhabited by a large population, was a sanctuary or a center of pilgrimage where people from the region or perhaps even from the most distant areas of Cuzco gathered. The structures which the archaeologists discovered and uncovered demonstrate the existence of a complete social life, that is, with all of the elements common to the interaction of social groups, with their hierarchies, standards and values. There is nothing which leads one to believe that the organization was different from that of the other large Inca settlements in Cuzco and outlying areas. On the contrary, during these years, Machu Picchu, as Ollantaytambo, was an area of agricultural production. This is demonstrated by the carefully designed terraces. Furthermore, there are signs of mining exploration and textile work. It is not at all difficult to believe, but rather is quite evident, that there must have been trade with non-Inca groups from the jungle. Or at least, one can imagine collective undertakings which made it possible to take advantage of the flora and fauna of the mountain summit and the virgin wood. What is known of the life of the Incas who sought refuge in Espíritu Pampa, in the company of the Augustinian friars, testifies to the possibility of Inca survival in these hot, humid lands.

Archaeological research and the history of Machu Picchu

During the memorable days from 1911 to 1915 in which Bingham was discovering the immense Inca structures in the Machu Picchu region and up until the present times, many research projects have been undertaken which detected important settlements and places, not only in the central area of what is presently included in the tourist visit to Machu Picchu, but also in a vast area which testifies to a region which was inhabited and cultivated since pre-Hispanic times, particularly in the Inca period.

Bingham did not return to Machu Picchu until 1948, when the political authorities gave his name to the road which leads to the archaeological site. Prior to this date, in 1941, the archaeologist Julio C. Tello, along with other researchers, explored the area which today is known with the name of Wiñay Wayna. Furthermore, he designed the popular Inca Trail which is traveled every year by thousands of tourists. Maintenance of the site and the area have led to new structures in the central complex other than those which Bingham and Tello discovered.

In the area near Machu Picchu, as well as in the areas surrounding the Aobamba and Urubamba rivers, there are undoubtedly signs of Inca occupation which time has not erased completely. All of this suggests a large region connected by roads and paths to the traditional populations of Cuzco and, through Cuzco, to the entire Andean territory.

«This was the abode, this is the place:
Here the wide grains of corn ascended
and were lowered again like red hailstones.
Here the golden thread was sheared from the vicuna
to clothe their loves, their tombs, their mothers,
the king, prayers, warriors».
(Pablo Neruda, p. 29).

Before embarking on the Machu Picchu roadway, one must bear in mind that the names attributed to the buildings, structures and details of the archaeological site are contemporary names given by explorers, archaeologists and historians. There is no written information to support them. Many of these names are based on interpretations which presently are considered completely false such as those which refer to Machu Picchu as a «citadel» or «military fortress» or «refuge of the Incas». There is not the slightest trace of such an intention in the architectural design of the place.

Therefore, it is advisable to discard these names spread by military or religious interpretations because if the visitor clings to them it will be very difficult for him or her to understand what is represented by the buildings, design and space. To help the visitor to situate himself in the literature as a whole on Machu Picchu, we have conserved these names even while affirming that they are erroneous or not very believable. The reader will know how to grant them their rightful importance.

Many visitors may ask if Machu Picchu was not a «city» in the sense which is usually given to this word, that is, a settlement with a significant population and with all of the goods and services which most people required for life in common.

Cuzco is a clear example of an urban area because of its size and design. The same can not be said of Machu Picchu. Its location, as well as what can be deduced from the measurement of the area, with approximately 200 structures, indicate that it could not hold a population greater than one thousand inhabitants. In this sense, neither is it very appropriate to consider that Machu Picchu had the urban character which many attribute to it.

What can be stated about Machu Picchu and verified by visitors to the area is the careful and harmonious architectural design, which takes maximum advantage of the space and physical conditions it offers. There is not the least doubt that there was clearly a desire to define the limits of the settlement and use the local resources to transform the area into a space inhabited in communion with nature and with the values and standards of Inca society. Since the rainy season in this area is extremely harsh, there are only three months a year in which the rain is less frequent and heavy. In choosing this place, the Incas equipped themselves with all elements which would ensure its permanent nature. In this sense, it can be said that the decision to occupy this area was made by the Inca elites. It is evident that Machu Picchu expresses the Inca desire for social and political expansion and for religious power, supported by settlements connected by roads which allowed economic as well as social interchanges between wide geographic areas of the Andes, particularly between those which had been built in the Yucay valley along the length of the watercourses where the mighty waters of the Vilcanota river reign. In Machu Picchu, after they flow through the region, these waters are referred to with the name Urubamba.

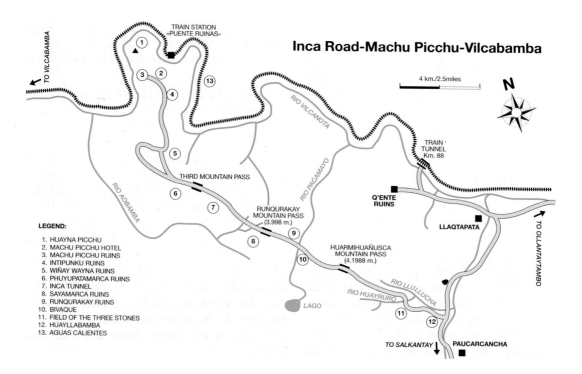

Inca Road-Machu Picchu-Vilcabamba

4 km./2.5miles

TRAIN STATION «PUENTE RUINAS»

TO VILCABAMBA

RIO VILCANOTA

RIO PACAMAYO

RIO AOBAMBA

THIRD MOUNTAIN PASS

RUNQURAKAY MOUNTAIN PASS (3.998 m.)

HUARMIHUAÑUSCA MOUNTAIN PASS (4.1988 m.)

TRAIN TUNNEL Km. 88

Q'ENTE RUINS

LLAQTAPATA

TO OLLANTAYTAMBO

RIO LLULLUCHA

RIO HUAYRURO

LAGO

TO SALKANTAY

PAUCARCANCHA

LEGEND:

1. HUAYNA PICCHU
2. MACHU PICCHU HOTEL
3. MACHU PICCHU RUINS
4. INTIPUNKU RUINS
5. WIÑAY WAYNA RUINS
6. PHUYUPATAMARCA RUINS
7. INCA TUNNEL
8. SAYAMARCA RUINS
9. RUNQURAKAY RUINS
10. BIVAQUE
11. FIELD OF THE THREE STONES
12. HUAYLLABAMBA
13. AGUAS CALIENTES

2. Travelling to Machu Picchu

There are several different ways to visit Machu Picchu: on foot, along the Inca Trail (which is possibly the most interesting alternative), by train from the city of Cuzco to Aguas Calientes, or by helicopter from the Cuzco airport to Aguas Calientes. Those who choose the first alternative may return by either of the other two, although the latter is the most expensive.

The Inca Trail
The route known as the Inca Trail (*El Camino del Inca* or *Camino Inca*) takes visitors from the city of Cuzco to Machu Picchu. This trail covers approximately 40 km and has a very well-documented history. The research conducted, from Bingham up until the present, has led to an itinerary which allows access to the archaeological site and the summit as well as all of the other areas which start from the lands bordering the Vilcanota and move away from the Yucay valley. More precisely, the starting point for visitors is kilometre 88 on the Cuzco-Quillabamba railway line, which is referred to as

The Inca Trail, at the point referred to as Kilometre 88, on the railway line between Cuzco and Quillabamba. At the beginning of the route the traveler follows the Vilcanota river and the railway line which leads to Machu Picchu.

Qoriwayrachina. The present tourist excursions prefer to begin their route starting at Chilca, located a bit earlier. Nevertheless, the location and route of the ancient trail are located in the place referred to as Llaqtapata, where there are ancient terraces and the town of the same name. This was the ancient starting point, or at least that which was used in pre-Hispanic times, which led towards Machu Picchu. Gradually, with the river at one's feet, the walker ascends through the Cusichaca valley, crossing the lands cultivated by the Augustinian friars and researched by the present archaeological work.

Today, the Inca Trail is followed by travelers from all over the world who, with backpacks or by leasing the services of the carriers from Ollantaytambo, embark on this walk which takes three days to reach Machu Picchu.

The trip through Runqurakay, with the view of the snow-capped peaks of Wakay Willka and the waters of Pacasmayo, can be stopped a few moments to visit the constructions in circular form, not very frequent in the Inca architecture. The semi-circle uses the area of the clearing which faces towards Warmiwañusca. Perhaps Hiram Bingham knew this place. The 1941 expedition, led by Paul Fejos, mentions Runcu Raccay, and describes and names the constructions in the form of a complete circle.

Although Machu Picchu is located at a height of 2,350 m above sea level –lower than the city of Cuzco (3,400 m)– along the Inca Trail the walker will surpass heights which reach up to a maximum of 4,200 m. Travelers who follow this route on foot usually take the local train, which leaves at dawn from the San Pedro station, to the aforementioned km 88. At this point, the route on foot to Machu Picchu begins. The natural scenery which dominates the trip to the Machu Picchu area is especially impressive because of the balance between the natural world and the Inca architecture. At dusk or dawn, framed by the snow-capped peaks at altitudes over 6,000 m –such as Salkantay, Huamantay, as well as others– the forest, the valleys, and the variety of flora and fauna in the scenery offer a continuous spectacle of fascination and mystery. Undoubtedly, if one's physical fitness allows him or her to do so, the Inca Trail is the best way to approach Machu Picchu.

Walkers on the Inca Path at Machu Picchu.

In Phuyupatamarca, the Inca Trail shows the traveler a unit of constructions in a strategic location with an imposing view over the valley of the Urubamba river. The area is more developed than Runqurakay. It is mentioned and named by Paul Fejos who, in 1940, explored the area for two months. Bingham had also passed through here without stopping. The traveler can enjoy the scenery and admire the beauty which surrounds it, from the peaks of Salkantay to the waters of Urubamba which flow rapidly towards Machu Picchu.

Close view of the unit of constructions in Phuyupatamarca, located in the area which Fejos named «high route», in contrast with the route of the other trail through the ruins, referred to as «low route». Both trails lead to the baths. There are six small lodges in a square shape with an opening on one side. The waters are channeled from the upper part of the construction.

The circular shape of the walls borders the natural area of the slope. As other areas which can be found along the Inca Trail, Phuyupatamarca shows signs of ritual and agricultural activities. The baths probably served as the former, although they also channeled the water towards the terraces.

Part of the extraordinary terraces of Wiñay Wayna, following the circular shape of the stream. The vegetation covers a vast expanse of similar constructions. The agricultural importance of the area is noteworthy. The high number of baths, more than those which exist in Machu Picchu itself, also suggest ritual practices, or simply concern for the use of water which flowed from the peaks and the springs of the stream.

Wiñay Wayna, with typical Inca architecture and with nineteen baths which are located beyond the houses, on the upper part of the panoramic view, indicates that we are approaching Machu Picchu. Although it is not marked, from the ruins the traveler can see, behind the hills, the hydroelectric power station which was built in 1960, and the Choquesuysuy ruins, explored in 1940, in times of the Fejos expedition.

Drawbridge along the Inca Trail, near Machu Picchu.

The route of the Inca Trail runs along the length of a wide diversity of Andean scenery. Besides the archaeological sites, with their multiple structures which are visited along the trail, the walkers pass through flat lands with thick vegetation, cross over high mountains and can distinguish the high snow-capped peaks and wooded mountains.

Views of the Inca Path.

Many of the sections along the Inca Trail are in a good state of conservation. For the construction of the flights of steps and roadways, the Incas used stone slabs carved for such purposes.

The carriers which groups of tourists and agencies hire to transport the travel equipment for travelers mostly come from the towns of Willoq, which is located above Ollantaytambo, and belong to the Association of Carriers of Cuzco. Traditionally dedicated to shepherding of the Andean camelidae and the cultivation of potatoes, the relations with tourism which they have experienced for several years are changing their ancient customs.

Andean camelidae on the Inca Trail.

With the view of Machu Picchu in the background, the landscape from the archaeological ruins of Intipunku along the Inca trail are the promontory which announces that the end of the trail is near.

The Inca Path,
near the Machu
Picchu citadel.

Lovely and varied scenery can be seen from the train which joins the city of Cuzco to Machu Picchu.

Journey by train

To travel by train to Machu Picchu, PERURAIL, the company that operates the Southern Railways, offers a wide variety of services which cover the needs of the different types of travellers to the former Inca citadel or the nearby area.

1. To take the so-called INCA ROUTE –Cuzco/Machu Piccu/Cuzco– the train departs from the San Pedro station. One can choose between different options: a) The Inca Service, which offers the most complete and comfortable service of all those available; b) Autovagón Service, which is the fastest and most comfortable, as well as the most suitable for photography buffs, due to the large windows this train is equipped with; c) Inexpensive Tourism/Backpacker Express, which is the most economical means of travel, that has been created recently for travellers who enjoy adventure tourism. The train is equipped with suitable shelves in order to accommodate the camping equipment that these passengers often carry.

2. There is another route that also leads to Machu Picchu. It is similar to the previous one, but shorter. It is referred to as the OLLANTA ROUTE –Ollantaytambo/Machu Picchu/Ollantaytambo– and begins in the main intermediate station, Ollanta. There are two different ways to take this route: a) by the Ferrostal Service, which has coaches equipped with large windows that are ideal for photography buffs; b) by the Backpacker Cerrojo, which is more economical than the previous option. This service has been created recently. It is also designed for adventuresome passengers who, after spending the night in the Sacred Valley, would like to travel to Machu Picchu from the Ollanta station.

3. POROY-MACHU PICCHU/MACHU PICCHU-POROY ROUTES: The Poroy station is located 18 km. from Cuzco, right in the Urubamba valley. This official station allows passengers and travel agencies to choose between the usual winding route, which takes an hour longer in both directions, and a shorter route departing from or arriving at Poroy (add a 20 minutes drive to or from Cuzco). PeruRail is planning to terminate the construction of a train turntable to offer a Poroy-Machu

Picchu-Poroy direct line by mid 2001. Nevertheless, the traditional winding route shall still be offered as an alternative.

Depending on the means of transportation and the time of day that one chooses to travel to Machu Picchu, there are trains which depart for Machu Picchu starting at dawn and during the early morning hours.

These trains take 40-90 minutes to travel to or from the Aguas Caliente station. The Aguas Caliente station is located in a small town near the Machu Picchu citadel. There are several shops, restaurants and different possibilities of lodging for travellers who decide to spend the night here. Such a stay also allows them to enjoy the impressive views of Machu Picchu and its environs at dawn and dusk. Some also choose to travel on foot between Aguas Calientes and the Machu Picchu citadel. This takes about an hour. However, usually the trip is made by bus. The return trip to the city of Cuzco is available in the mid-afternoon or at dusk.

Travellers can also organize the trip to Machu Picchu on their own. One can purchase tickets in the main reservation station at Wanchaq station or through a travel agency. Most of the travel agencies are located in the Plaza de Armas in Cuzco or the surrounding area. They offer itineraries which include a guide and all services, including the option of picking up travellers at their respective hotels and taking them to the station.

The visit by train to Machu Picchu can be done in a day, departing from Cuzco at dawn and returning in the mid-afternoon or at dusk. Nevertheless, this form of travel is extremely tiresome and hasty.

One of the most noteworthy attractions of Machu Picchu is being able to leisurely gaze at the citadel under the wide range of daylight that falls on each corner of the archaeological site as the day progresses, especially during the rainy season.

Travel by helicopter

This is the option which is chosen least frequently. It is also the most expensive way to travel to Machu Picchu,

The wide range of colors and the arrangement of the plots of land in the geographic surroundings of Chinchero, visible from the helicopter which travels from Cuzco to Aguas Calientes, seem to be inspired by the rich textile designs of the Andes, which used native plants for the colors.

Aerial panoramic view of the Sacred Valley of the Incas on the trip by helicopter from Cuzco to Aguas Calientes.

Flying over the Urubamba river in the trip by helicopter from Cuzco to Aguas Calientes.

although it does have some attractions. There are some who combine this form of travel with the Inca Trail or the trip by train. The flight takes half an hour and tickets can be purchased at any travel agency in Cuzco or Aguas Calientes, or at the entry to Machu Picchu. The helicopter leaves the airport and reaches the Aguas Calientes station. From there travel to Machu Picchu is by bus.

The Vilcanota river as it flows through Aguas Calientes, town located at Kilometre 110 of the Cuzco-Quillabamba railway line. This is the place where most of the inns which serve as lodging for visitors to Machu Picchu are located. Restaurants, agencies, businesses and the hot springs which rise from the underground can also be found here.

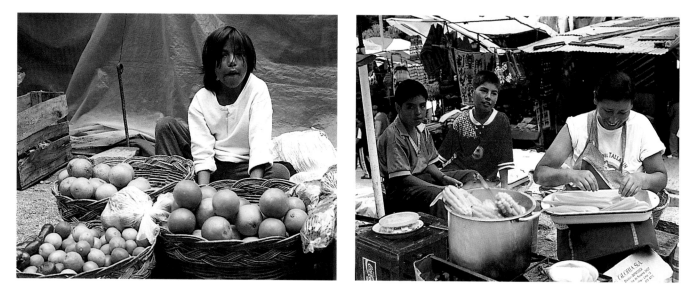

The people of Aguas Calientes, who are mostly from different areas of the Andean mountains, all live directly or indirectly from the influx of tourists which visit Machu Picchu each day. In this sense, the businesses and the different stands of street vendors which can be found in the area offer a varied and colorful mixture of products, including the everyday consumption of their usual inhabitants as well as other items which are of more interest to tourists.

Route of access, along a winding roadway, to the citadel of Machu Picchu, starting at the Puente Ruinas train station, next to the Vilcanota river. This route was inaugurated in 1948 by Hiram Bingham and bears his name.

Panoramic view of the land where the agricultural activities took place and an adjacent area of constructions of the citadel which are separated from the terraces by a dry trench. This area accounts for approximately 20 hectares.

3. Machu Picchu

All of the information available about Machu Picchu is the result of archaeological research, based on the discovery by Hiram Bingham and later continued up until the present by the work of enlarging and maintaining the site. It must also be remembered that most of the descriptions of the area and the different structures are based on the comparison with other Inca archaeological sites about which, in some cases, there is written information. Finally one must bear in mind that one of the most interesting dimensions of the Machu Picchu settlement is the fact that it is a wide area occupied by the Incas where there is no evidence of the existence of cultures prior to the Incas. Therefore, in Machu Picchu visitors find a typically Incan expression of the organization of space and the social, political

and religious system which prevailed in this area. It is certainly difficult to fully understand the lines drawn in the design of the area. We will try to do so with the maximum accuracy and avoiding imaginary explanations which rather than offering help in understanding the area, tend to be dominated by fantasies and esotericism of bad taste.

Inca agriculture: land and water

The images we have reviewed up until now show several views of the terraces in different places which lead to Machu Picchu along the Inca Trail. This is one of the most noteworthy facts of the visit. Throughout the vast territory which makes up the map of Machu Picchu, there are clear signs of the Inca concern to make the most of the streams and watercourses. The intense agricultural activity in this area served to feed the population which inhabited the valley. In this sense, the carefully designed terraces of Machu Picchu imitate the features of those in the Yucay valley and nearby areas. Ollantaytambo, where the Inca Trail begins, offers an example of this.

Land in the agricultural sector with small constructions which were used by those in charge of the sector. The terraces, on the lower part, served as retaining walls for the areas with a steep slope which underwent heavy rains during the rainy season.

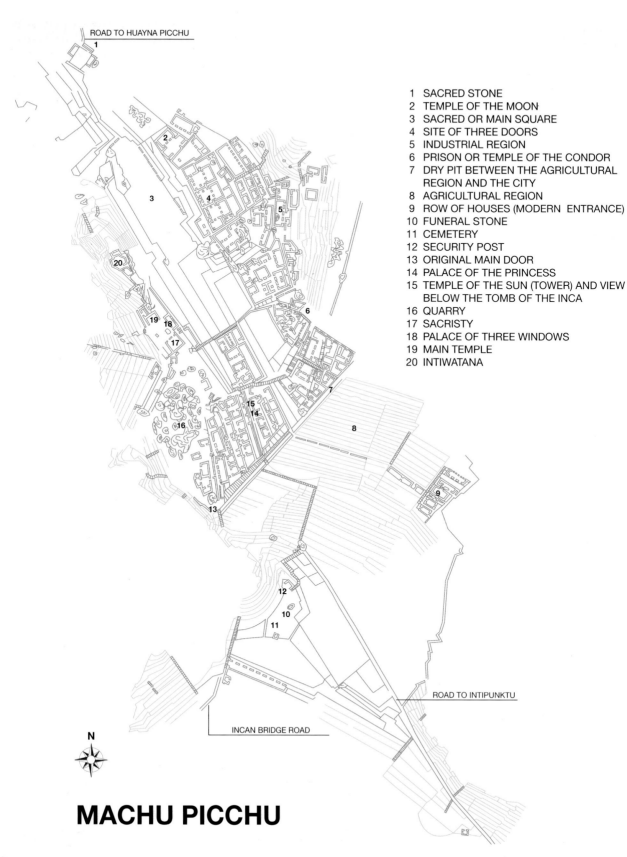

ROAD TO HUAYNA PICCHU

1 SACRED STONE
2 TEMPLE OF THE MOON
3 SACRED OR MAIN SQUARE
4 SITE OF THREE DOORS
5 INDUSTRIAL REGION
6 PRISON OR TEMPLE OF THE CONDOR
7 DRY PIT BETWEEN THE AGRICULTURAL
  REGION AND THE CITY
8 AGRICULTURAL REGION
9 ROW OF HOUSES (MODERN ENTRANCE)
10 FUNERAL STONE
11 CEMETERY
12 SECURITY POST
13 ORIGINAL MAIN DOOR
14 PALACE OF THE PRINCESS
15 TEMPLE OF THE SUN (TOWER) AND VIEW
   BELOW THE TOMB OF THE INCA
16 QUARRY
17 SACRISTY
18 PALACE OF THREE WINDOWS
19 MAIN TEMPLE
20 INTIWATANA

ROAD TO INTIPUNKTU

INCAN BRIDGE ROAD

N

MACHU PICCHU

Due to its shape and location, the name of Funeral Rock has been given to this stone carved in an outlying area near the Watchman's House, where remains of bones have been found. This area was a cemetery and the carved rock, with its flight of steps and rings in the pierced stone, was the place where offerings and ritual funeral activities took place.

The Watchman's House or Surveillance Post was the name given to a unique structure which includes a roof with two slopes, three walls and several windows, located on the peak of the agricultural sector, above the terraces. Its location makes one think of an observation post for the overall view of the entire area visible from this place.

Constructions near the terraces and, in the background, a slightly cloudy view of Huayna-Picchu.

Panoramic view over the set of buildings located in the agricultural area. The walls of the terraces are solid and the stone is cut. The angle of the slope required solid walls and the water from the springs and the rains needed fast, unobstructed canals.

The watercourses also played an essential role in all Inca activity. The agitated Andean geography created many problems for irrigation of the land. From early times, the Andean cultures faced this problem and constructed networks of canals which allowed water to be transported from the springs and small lakes to barren land or areas far from their origin. Strictly speaking, it was not exclusively an Inca activity. Today we can state that it existed for many centuries prior to the arrival of the Incas who, as those who had preceded them, knew how to take advantage of this traditional knowledge.

There are no exact conclusions on the purpose of such

Panoramic view of Machu Picchu from the agricultural region.

Door of entry to the place, located on the southern end of the inhabited or urban area, with thick walls and cut stone. The shape is rectangular. Bingham, on his first expedition, noticed successive changes in the construction of the entryway.

Panoramic view of the citadel which includes the Main Temple and the Palace of the Three Windows, with access to the hill where Intiwatana is located, by the flight of steps made of carved stone.

Main Temple. Building with three walls which covers a wide area, with a length of 11 m and a width of 8 m. The three walls contain niches where the mummies which always accompanied the Incas were kept. The altar is located in the background, next to the central wall.

Detail of the side wall of the Main Temple with finely smoothed stone and one of the niches clearly marked. On the angle which joins the upper part of the wall with the lower part which ascends, there is an opening where the ends of the beams which supported the roof can be inserted. The snow-capped peaks of the mountain range visible on the horizon are also noteworthy.

The name of Palace or Temple of the Three Windows is used to refer to a rectangular building where three finely worked windows and two blind openings can be found (it could be said that there were five windows). As regards this building, some archaeologists cite the tale of the Ayar brothers, mythical ancestors of the Incas, which says that the heroes had left through the three windows, in the town of Pacaritambo (Cuzco).

The Temple or Palace of the Three Windows displays the architecture and the smoothness of the most finished stone of Machu Picchu. It location near what is referred to as the Main Square supports the idea of a building with great social, political and religious importance. It may have been used for religious purposes. Nevertheless, there is no reason to believe that the architectural shape is related to the tale of the origin of the mythical ancestors of the Incas, the Ayar brothers, and much less so to an exclusively religious function of this area.

Close view of one of the windows where one can see the fine smoothness of the stone and the millimetric fit of each stone which forms the window in the wall of the building. In the background, partial view of the Main Square.

Intiwatana. This is referred to as Intiwatana, name which brings to mind a popular tradition which says that «the sun is tied» to series of architectural structures located on the highest point in the center of Machu Picchu, which is reached by climbing up 78 finely carved stone steps. The courtyard includes a quadrangular prism with a height of 36 centimeters, facing north-west and south-east, which suggests the idea of the astronomical functions of the place, with each pebble of the square pointing towards the four cardinal points. According to the observations made, it seems that the movement of the sun and the shade on the quadrangular stone may have indicated the solstices and the equinoxes. Nevertheless, it may also have simply been an altar for ritual activities located in the surroundings of the courtyard and similar buildings.

agricultural activity. Based on tradition, we can assume that corn was part of the agricultural cycle. This was also the case of the variety of tubers grown in the mountainous area, such as the potato which the Andes made known to the entire world. It would not be strange if, in some of the hotter regions, coca leaves were also cultivated, as their ritual use was even more widespread during Inca times.

As regards water, archaeologists and explorers indicate that the canals from the springs were directed towards the ritual baths, in order to introduce the watercourse in some small square-shaped constructions where it seems that those who approached the region could be purified. This is a credible hypothesis. Throughout the area there are examples of fountains which come out of the canals constructed for irrigation. Along the way, these waters might also have been used for other objectives, including that of ritual baths. In the 16th century chronicles, there are references to purification practices in which during certain times of the year the population or the political or religious elites conducted rites in which water played an essential role. The place where the watercourses intersect represents an important point in the pre-Hispanic symbolic world. This is the case regardless of whether the water which is flung against the slopes which lean over the land originates in rivers or brooks or springs. The meeting place of these waters was considered an important symbolic area in pre-Hispanic Andean cultures. This was also the case of the other watercourses which share this practical ambivalence, that of being useful for agriculture and of being object of a ritual activity.

Social organization of space

The different constructions of Machu Picchu which the traveler finds along the Inca Trail have been designed based on a specific notion of occupying the space. We have access to this information from other constructed areas occupied by the Incas. It is clear that all of the notions employed in this sense derive from more or less credible hypotheses, and at times from the false use of space. They are not the consequence of descriptions by eyewitnesses from the 16th century as such testimonies, as mentioned previously, have not been available up until now. The texts by Bingham and contemporary archaeologists speak to us about houses or large fortified watchtowers, the industrial sector, royal apartments, funeral altars and stones and other architectural details. One must bear in mind the following: all of these statements are approximations regarding an area which can not be fully understood to the extent in which it is not documented or supported by ancient testimonies. This means that the present name of

This view, which centers on the Sacred Square or Main Square, emphasizes Intiwatana hill and the buildings of the area which was referred to as the «hanan» or high area. This area later extends towards the right, with the Square and the «hurin», or lower area.

View of the heart of the citadel, with fog in the background which covers the hill of Huayna Picchu like a delicate veil. Some explorers claim that the citadel was divided into two halves: this view includes the area considered «hurin» (lower area), in contrast with «hanan» (high area) in front.

Panoramic view of the sector referred to as «hurin» or lower area. The flight of steps borders the buildings and leads to the different courtyards or wide platforms.

Partial view of the enclosure or platform with the floors of the surrounding area and the steps which border and connect the main buildings which had known functions.

41

Trail which leads to the flight of steps which borders the central buildings in the area also referred to as «hurin» or lower area, not so much in the physical sense of the word but rather in the social sense.

Palace of the Mortar, with a fine stone finish, niches and mortar in the middle of the area.

The Indian Temple of the Niches. Wall with niches seated on bare rock, at a slope with a flight of steps. It is assumed that the mummies which underwent long ceremonies were tied in the niches with holes.

43

Bingham referred to this extraordinary unit as the prison area. But the figure on the floor with the shape which resembles the head and neck of a condor suggested to explorers the image of the condor.

Magnificent expression of Inca use of bare rock in the architectural shapes.

Rock figure in the shape of a condor head and neck.

these places is not totally erroneous. Nevertheless, one must take into account that they are place-names designated by archaeology, which is approximate and hypothetical.

Having clarified this point, it is evident that in the space occupied by the Incas there were constructions which housed different sectors of the population. There is a perfectly clear division between the agricultural area and the area occupied by the population. But, having affirmed and recognized this principle, all further statements are purely hypothetical. What was the use of the small house which the Incas designated as the «watchman's house», located on the pinnacle of the terraces of Machu Picchu? What role was played by that which was referred to as the Intiwatana stone or the sun clock? What arguments can be defended as regards the hypothesis of an urban architectural design based on the astronomic position of the stones or constructions? What particular aspects are indicated by the «funeral rock»? How can we explain the existence of human remains which have led to the erroneous belief that the female population was superior to the male? All of

Temple of the Sun or Tower, discovered by Bingham. Although it is not frequent in Inca architecture, there are circular and semicircular shapes. This is an excellent example of this design.

these and other questions can be posed and, in fact, have been done so when it is a matter of knowing with accuracy what all of these important constructions are, where the carefully designed architecture, and the design appropriate for the objectives sought by the Incas, are not lacking. The most obvious question is as follows: What objectives did the Incas pursue with the construction and development of a living area in Machu Picchu?

Looking closely at the design of the area, the presence of shapes and architectural masses which are typical of the Incas can be detected. For example, the stone known with the name of Intiwatana. The shape as well as the location in the occupation of the space as a whole repeats a model found in the Pisac ruins, in the Yucay valley, and in other areas of the Andes. Furthermore, the «three windows» which are visible in

Panoramic view of the Temple of the Sun or Fortified Tower with the flight of steps which connects the different buildings in the architectural unit.

Royal Tomb. There is a cavern on the lower part of the rock supporting the so-called Temple of the Sun or Fortified Tower which has been carefully designed and adorned. It suggests the idea of a mausoleum, although there is no archaeological evidence which confirms this.

Excellent sample of the superimposed use of stones in the shape of a door in the Temple of the Sun. The holes in some of the stones bring to mind the custom which existed in the Temple of the Sun or Qoricancha, in the city of Cuzco. Some texts from the sixteenth and seventeenth centuries speak of precious metals which were inserted in these holes to decorate the area.

Walls, windows and niches taking advantage of the carved stone in the Temple of the Sun or Fortified Tower.

Fountains and baths. Very near the structures which surround what is known as the Royal Palace or Temple of the Sun or Fortified Tower, in the southern area, there are fountains and water canals, carved in the rock with their drainage system and walls which retain the water and then allow it to filter in order to provide water for the system of agricultural irrigation.

The channeling of water was a subject of constant concern for pre-Hispanic civilizations. The attention dedicated to channeling and taking full advantage of the underground springs is especially noteworthy.

Because of their shape and fine finish it is probable that these fountains were also used for ritual purposes.

Royal Palace. This is the name used to designate the series of buildings which offer access to a narrow passageway which opens out to a courtyard where several rooms are found. The imagination of the archaeologists attributed several functions to these rooms: «wayranas» or rooms with three walls with niches and chambers for the main master, smaller rooms, and roofs which most likely had two slopes. The overall impression is of carefully designed and wide space in which the walls are thick and the stone finishes are very smooth.

the wall of some buildings. On several occasions, archaeologists have discovered this type of design. Also, of course, the shape of the niches where it is known that the Incas placed their mummies as in small domestic or ritual altars. All of these coincidences between the architectural design of Machu Picchu and the Inca structures as a whole throughout the Andes grant a basis to the opinions proposed by archaeologists on the use of the buildings and the constructed area as a whole.

Bingham pointed out the existence of two sectors, that of the Inca high class, and that of the common or popular classes. This brings to mind the division which the writer Inca Garcilaso de la Vega used for the city of Cuzco, the high part or *hanan*, and the lower part or *hurin*. There is a central type of architecture which corresponds to each of these areas: that of the masters is more carefully designed and worked on than that of the popular classes. Also, the architectural unit which is found on the side of the terraces, crowned with a small house on the peak, referred to as the Watchman's House, as dwelling place or lodge for those responsible for the maintenance of the terraces and the agricultural activities conducted in the area. The highest part of this section includes broader spaces than those which are below, and the latter of these are designed for restraint and not for cultivation. In this high sector, the presence of graves and cut stone is especially noteworthy. Here what archaeologists refer to as the Funeral Rock is found, following the Inca model of construction, which placed the cemeteries on the periphery of the construction. The aristocratic or urban sector includes that which is referred to as the Temple of the Sun, the Royal Palace and the Royal Tomb, the Plaza Mayor, the Intiwatana, the Temple of the Three Windows. Next to the Temple of the Sun there are fountains with ritual baths and what is referred to as the prison area or the architectural group of the Condor. On the lower part of the sector, there is a cemetery, and not far away, in the direction of Huayna Picchu, is located what is known with the name of Workshop or House-Workshop. Continuing in this same direction, there is the construction of the Temple of the Moon or the Sacred Rock.

Inca architecture and ecology

Although speaking about ecology is transferring to another era a notion which was not used at that time, the Inca concern for conserving the physical and natural characteristics in their place is a credible notion. In this sense, it is also not inappropriate to use the term «ecology» to refer to a noteworthy fact which is quite clear in Machu Picchu: the existence of a perfect harmony between the architectural conception and design, and the physical and natural characteristics found there. Cut stones; scarce land; abundant rainfall; underground springs; strong, cold winds and storms, which demanded appropriate protection for the perma-

Flight of steps. One of the most spectacular architectural motifs in the citadel of Machu Picchu is that of the flight of steps. The sloping angle of the land and the use of slopes with steep angles was the physical area imposed on the Incas. Therefore, as in evident in the slanted planes in the shape of a ladder, the Inca were especially concerned about the construction of a network of narrow paths of stone and steps in Machu Picchu.

Walkway and crossing in the shape of a flight of steps. This takes advantage of the slope of the land in the design of a wide walkway with well polished stone and access to the buildings.

The architecture and the urban arrangement of the space which the Incas developed show great wisdom in the use of the stones, and in the precise adaptation which each type of stone could provide for its objectives. The Inca Trail and the citadel of Machu Picchu display a wide variety of shapes of stones, probably formed by stones from the nearby land. In this sense, here is a sample which includes the smoothest stones, which were used for lodging the most outstanding figures of the Incas, or areas for ritual activities; wall constructions with carved stone which are not especially smooth; primitive stone walls which were used to organize the space and as a light retaining wall for the slope of the land; retaining walls made of unworked, rough stones etc.

nent population. As a result of all of these characteristics, the term ecology is an appropriate expression for the work performed by the Incas in the place. Likewise it is not an abuse of language to state that it offers an example to follow in terms of conserving the properties of a place or its areas, of respecting them and making them known. Undoubtedly, for all of these reasons, the visit to Machu Picchu makes a strong impression on visitors, who leave the area with the emotions of someone who has physically and spiritually experienced the singular experience of full communion between spirit and earth.

The use of local granite is one of the most typical shapes in the structures of Machu Picchu. The Incas took advantage of the most minimum support offered by the physical surroundings. This smooth stone with steps can be compared with that of the Funeral Rock (p. 33) and with other Inca structures in the region.

Set of structures on a slope with use of the slope of the land to raise walls which also served as retaining walls. Note the semicircular design of one of the walls and the wall which protects the structure of the upper building, suggesting the idea of a courtyard or open space with its own architectural design.

Stone platform carved in rock. This is another example which can be seen in the landscape.

The doors or entryways with rectangular shapes alternate with trapezoidal shapes. The slope of the land allows panoramic views of the areas nearby or far from the door. Some of them seem to lead to emptiness, as though they were simply openings meant for ventilation. In other cases, some of them are arranged so that they form an aligned unit as suggested by this rectangular shape as well as that which can be seen below, in the adjacent building.

Trail in the shape of a corridor between two sets of structures with a crossing. Given the importance of the rainy season in Machu Picchu, the trail also allowed the water to flow quickly and the drying of the land, in many cases with a steep slope.

Trapezoidal door. The trapezium is the design which best defines Inca architecture. It was preceded by rectangular shapes used by the Tiawanaku culture in the Lake Titicaca area, several centuries prior to the construction of Machu Picchu.

Sacred Rock. Name given to a very lovely rock, with a height of three metres and seven metres at the base. The pedestal measures approximately 30 cm. Depending on the angle from which it is viewed, the rock may seem to represent a feline image or an architectural image of the nearby mountain area.

The highest part of Huayna-Picchu.

Panoramic view of the route which ascends from the Puente Ruinas train station to the settlements of Machu Picchu, and complete view of the citadel, viewed from the upper part of Huayna-Picchu.

The imposing and watchful presence of Putucusi hill, framed by the Vilcabamba mountain range, can be seen from the trail which leads from Aguas Calientes to Machu Picchu, as well as from different places in the citadel. The climatic changes which normally take place throughout the day, especially in the rainy season, along with the changing patterns of light and clouds provides the hill with an extremely diversified appearance regardless of the place from which it is viewed.

Panoramic view of the present entrance to the citadel of Machu Picchu.

Panoramic view of Putucusi hill as seen from the agricultural sector of the Machu Picchu citadel.

Panoramic view of Putucusi hill from the traditional entry to the citadel.

Panoramic view of Urubamba canyon, as seen from Machu Picchu. The Cuzco-Quillabamba railway line runs parallel to the Vilcanota river, name which means dwelling place of the sun.

The Urubamba valley, viewed from the citadel of Machu Picchu.

Machu Picchu has lush vegetation. A simple lane or a narrow path offer varied flowers to the visitor. In contrast with the green color of the surroundings, the red tones are emphasized to balance the freshness of the meadows created by the high level of humidity in the atmosphere.

Flora of Machu Picchu

Machu Picchu not only offers visitors an impressive mountain range where the Incas built a town which was harmoniously designed, making the most of the resources offered by nature, even in the most minute details. Machu Picchu also displays an extraordinary variety of floral species which for many years have attracted the attention of specialists and visitors fascinated by the beauty of the shapes and the variety and shades of colors. Unfortunately, the presence of the influx of visitors poses several problems for these species, which are extremely sensitive to the disorganized presence of people eager to take home a reminder of their visit to the area.

The orchids, for example, are not unnoticed by the gaze of the tourists. Many visitors believe that the abundance of the local flora is endless. They are mistaken. The species are decreasing every day. There are no accurate studies on this subject. Some researchers point out that it is quite possible that there were three hundred species of orchids. A great effort must be made to save them. Other genuses which were the object of untimely cutting for many years have also been pointed out.

Each species has its own rhythm and time of duration. Some are nearly millimetric, whereas others have survived because of their size and shape. The height at which they can live and survive also plays an important role. Many of the variety of genuses are the product of the steep slope of the hills and the variety of climates and temperatures. The colors and the shapes reflect this.

The infinite variety of shapes and colors are surprising to the gaze. The pink colors abound in different genuses. Specimens emerge in the midst of resistant leaves which keep them alive for several days. Some genuses do not measure more than a few millimeters. The variety of orchids is noteworthy and many specialists know that Machu Picchu offers a great abundance of examples in this field. They may not last much longer. They seek refuge in the wood to survive or derive their own existence from this area.

End of the journey. In the mid-afternoon, at the Aguas Caliente station, the train sets out on the return trip to the city of Cuzco.

Contents

Bibliography

BINGHAM, Hiram. *Machu Picchu. A Citadel of the Incas*, Hacker Art Books, New York, 1979 (1930).

BUSE, Hermann. *Machu Picchu*, Nueva Crónica, Lima, 1961.

FEJOS, Paul. *Archaeological Explorations in the Cordillera Vilcamaba Southeastern Peru*, The Viking Fund, 1963.

GASPARINI, Graziano and Luise MARGOLIES. *Arquitectura inca,* Universidad Central de Venezuela, Caracas, 1977.

GLAVE, Luis Miguel and María Isabel REMY. *Estructura agraria y vida rural en una región andina. Ollantaytambo entre los siglos XVI y XIX*, Centro de Estudios Rurales Andinos «Bartolomé de las Casas», Cuzco, 1983.

HARDOY, Jorqe Enrique. *Ciudades precolombinas,* Buenos Aires, 1964.

NERUDA, Pablo. *Canto General*, Bruguera, Barcelona, 1980.

PARDO, Luis. *Machu Picchu: Una joya arquitectónica de los incas*, Cuzco, 1961.

TORD, Luis Enrique. *Guide to Machu Picchu*, Delfos Ediciones, s/f.

VALCÁRCEL, Luis E. *Machu Picchu*, Editorial Universitaria, Buenos Aires, 1964.

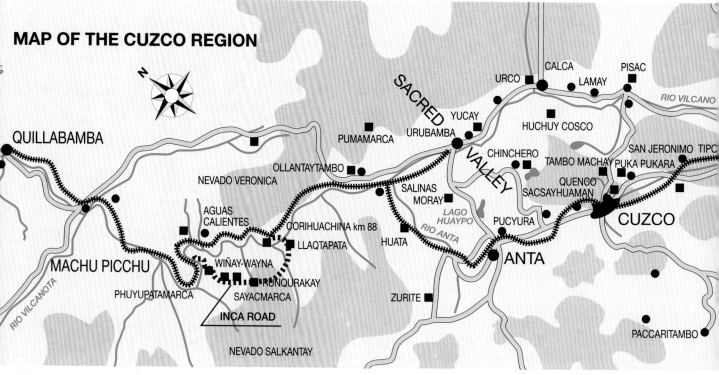

MAP OF THE CUZCO REGION